At the

Orchard

Published by The Child's World®, Inc.

Design and Production:
The Creative Spark, San Juan Capistrano, CA

Photos: © 1998 David M. Budd Photography
Illustrations: Robert Court

Library of Congress Cataloging-in-Publication Data
Sirimarco, Elizabeth 1966-
    At the orchard / by Elizabeth Sirimarco.
        p. cm.
    Summary: Briefly describes in simple text the work that goes on at
a fruit orchard and some of the equipment used there.
    ISBN 1-56766-576-4 (lib. reinforced : alk. paper)
    1. Orchards Juvenile literature. 2. Fruit-culture Juvenile literature. [1. Orchards.
2. Fruit culture.] I. Title.
SB357.2.S57 1999
634—dc21
                                                                              99-18807
                                                                                  CIP

At the
Orchard

Written by Elizabeth Sirimarco
Photos by David M. Budd

FIELD TRIPS

The Child's World®, Inc.

Let's go visit the **orchard!**

Hundreds of trees grow many kinds of fruit.

In the summer and fall, farmers pick the fruit.

This orchard is in Colorado!

Cherries are the first fruit to **ripen.**
They are all gone now.
Farmers pick peaches and pears in
July and August.

This orchard grows seven kinds of apples.
Now the Gala apples are ready to **harvest.**
Mmmmm! The apples smell good.

Shiny, red Gala apples taste sweet!

The farmer puts a bag over his shoulders.

Snap! Snap!

He puts the apples he picks in his bag.

Another worker makes boxes for the apples.

Picking apples is a lot of work!

The farmer climbs a ladder.

Now he can reach fruit at the very

top of the tree.

There are hundreds of different
kinds of apples grown all
around the world.

Another farmer has filled his bag.

He empties the apples into a big tub of water.

Plop! Plop! Plop!

Now the farmers take the apples out.

Little baskets make their job easier.

Drip! Drip!

They dry each and every apple.

Now the apples are shiny and clean.

The farmer puts the apples into a box.

Fuji apples are the last to be harvested. They are ready to pick in November.

All the boxes are full.

The farmer loads the boxes onto a **tractor.**

He drives the tractor down a hill.

The farmer unloads the boxes.

He stores them in a giant **cooler.**

Once fruit has been picked, it doesn't like to get too hot! Orchard workers keep fruit in a cooler until they take it to the market.

The farmer has other jobs to do.

First he will **plow** the orchard's fields.

The United States grows
more apples than any other
country in the world.

He drives by the wind machine.

The big machine can blow warm air across

the orchard on cold spring days.

Whoosh! Whoosh!

A wind machine keeps
blossoms from freezing if the
weather gets too cold. If the
blossoms freeze, there won't be
any fruit in the summertime.

Next the farmer checks the honeybees.

These white boxes are bee **hives.**

The bees produce honey in the hives.

Buzz! Buzz!

Finally it's time to sell the apples at the **farmer's market.** The orchard also sells honey and pears. Workers **weigh** fruit for a customer.

Let's take our apples home and bake a yummy pie!

EVER UPWARD
PLES
Excelsior Orchard
Certified Organic
Gala Apples
$150/lb
Bartlett Pears
Winter Pears
Honey
$350 sm jar
$600 Lg Jar

Glossary

cooler (KOO-lur) — A cooler is something that keeps other things cold. Farmers put fruit in a cooler before it goes to the market.

farmer's market (FAR-merz MAR-kit) — A farmer's market is a place where farmers sell the fruits and vegetables that they grow. Farmers sell apples at the farmer's market.

harvest (HAR-vest) — When a farmer harvests something, he picks it. Farmers harvest apples in autumn.

hives (HIVES) — Hives are containers where bees live. Bees make honey in their hives.

orchard (OAR-churd) — An orchard is a farm where people grow fruit. Farmers grow apples, cherries, and other fruits at an orchard.

plow (PLAU) — When farmers plow the soil, they move it around and break it up. Farmers plow the orchard's fields.

ripen (RIPE-n) — When foods ripen, they become ready to eat. Cherries are the first fruits to ripen at the orchard.

tractor (TRACK-tor) — A tractor is a machine that can move through fields and pull things. Farmers use tractors to carry the apples they pick.

weigh (WAY) — When you weigh something, you see how heavy it is. Workers weigh apples at the orchard.

Index

Elizabeth Sirimarco has written more than 20 books for young readers. She and her husband, photographer David Budd, live in Colorado.